Through Amy's Eyes

Through Amy's Eyes

Dreams, Visions,
and Inspirations

by
Amy Rose Powers

Compiled by
Darry E. Powers

Art Work by
Troy R.B. Powers

Through Amy's Eyes
Copyright © 1998 by
Amy Rose Powers

Library of Congress
Catalog Card Number: 98-091413

ISBN: 1-57579-111-0

ALL RIGHTS RESERVED.

No part of this book may be reproduced or transmitted in any form or by any means, electronic or mechanical, including photocopying, recording, or by any information storage and retrieval system, without permission in writing from the author.

Printed in United States of America

Introduction

Amy Rose Powers was born 20 April 1977 with serious health problems that indicated she may never walk. By the age of two she took her first steps. Born into a military family, she experienced many moves and with them a variety of people and places. Amy Rose wrote her first poem at the early age of seven, only one year before the separation of her parents through divorce. Her poetry seemed to be an outlet for the emotional trauma she experienced; yet much of her writing shows the inner faith and strength that, even as a young child, was able to find rainbows in an otherwise dismal world.

For the next decade, within Amy Rose's family she would face death (several close family members to include her Father when she was 16), financial hardship, life threatening illness (several close family members), suicide, and rape. Again she took pen in hand and poured her emotion onto paper.

Rising above the hardship and trauma that touched her life, Amy Rose graduated from High School in only three years and went on to college pursuing an education and career in criminal justice and law. Over the years she has bought gifts for needy children even when she has gone without, has given her last dollar at church on Sunday, and has stopped to buy a hamburger for a homeless man on a street corner. Amy Rose has volunteered for countless causes involving the needy, aged, handicapped, or underprivileged because her philosophy in life has always been that "yes, *one* person *can* make a difference."

But most importantly, she has touched the hearts of many. For it is *"Through Amy's Eyes"* that the world is seen not only as it is, but also "as it should be." Amy Rose has seen faith in the light of uncertainty, hope in the light of despair, and touched the hearts of others with love in time of sorrow. Even in her own times of hardship and trauma, she has been a ray of sunshine in the lives of her family, taken time out to extend a hand to a friend in need, and shouldered responsibility well beyond her years.

This book of Amy Rose's writing is being compiled by her family as a legacy to all of the hearts she has touched and all of those that will be touched by reading this book. It is a combination of her poetry and excerpts of some of the writings she has done. Perhaps it will give you strength in times of despair or the courage to face a new day. By seeing the world *"Through Amy's Eyes,"* we hope that it also will give you the inspiration and hope to see the world a little brighter.

Thank you Amy Rose, for all that you do, for all that you are, and for allowing us all to see the world a little brighter through your eyes.

We Love You
Your Mom and Brother

Dedication

To my family and friends
who have given me the love
that has given me the strength
and faith not only to survive
but to turn raindrops into rainbows.

Each one of you are
"Someone Special"

. . . Personal Reflections. . . . .

For Someone Special

It takes only one smile
    To offer someone a welcome...
And blessed be the person
    Who will share it.

It only takes one moment
    To be helpful and kind...
And blessed be the person
    Who will take it.

It only takes one joy
    To lift a saddened spirit...
And blessed be the person
    Who will give it.

It only takes one life
    To make a difference...
And blessed be the person
    Who will live it.

[Age 13]

. . . Personal Reflections. . . . .

The Bird

I see a bird come from above
   as the sun starts to rise
The bird is so full of love
   as I look at his little eyes.

He is so full of life
   as cute as you can be
He is no longer full of strife
   as I see him look down on me.

[Age 7]

Joy

Joy is the color of sunshine
It sounds like a flowing stream
The taste of a delicious, juicy orange
Joy smells like crisp fresh air
And looks like the beauty of a budding flower
Joy makes your heart feel brand new.

[Age 8]

... *Personal Reflections*. . . . .

Rock & Roll ♪♪

He is there for every dance
Every time you take a chance
He is there when you are blue
And when you are happy too.
He loves to sing. . .
And play "The Wild Thing"
He loves to play and really rocks...
Of course he is. . . our Jukebox!!

[Age 8]

...Personal Reflections........

["We have no money and times have been hard. Sometimes it is hard to put into words our feelings that are buried so deep. This isn't the greatest gift or poem in the world but it is all I have to give except for my love and thanks. Thank You, I Love You, and Happy Mother's Day." - Age 8]

Mom

The sun's hot and radiant glow,
The soft colors of a rainbow...
The rain, sleet, snow, and dew...
All remind me so much of you.

Soft music, gentle breeze,
From the mountains to the seas...
All remind me of a heart that's true...
Mom, they all remind me so much of you. [Age 8]

My Mother, My Friend

When I have a fear...
She's there to wipe each tear.
When I need a close friend...
My problems she always seems to mend.

When I can no longer stand...
She's there to lend her gentle hand.
With her bright shining smile
Stretching out over the miles.

She's always there...
Her face showing so much care.
She's a friend like no other...
This special friend is my mother.

[Age 12]

...Personal Reflections........

To You I Give

When I was helpless; you gave me your hand...
    I repaid you only with a "thank you;"
And when I fell; you helped me to stand...
    I repaid you, only with a smile.

When I was sad and you lent me your ears...
    I repaid you with a simple handshake.
Then I cried and you wiped away my tears...
    And I repaid you, only with a smile.

Now every day that you help me through...
    I know no words can ever express
All of my thanks for all that you do...
    So to you I give all of my love...
                    ... and a smile.

[Age 10]

. . . Personal Reflections. . . . .

Homebase
[Sights and sounds of a Junior High Homebase Room]

Shrill awakening ring
Slow muffle of students
Passing the teacher's muffled voice
Loud dreaded words
Annoying wet sneezes
Forceless yawns
Slow turning of notebooks
While an anonymous kyd tries to turn off the
                                                         light
Pop! Goes the window thrashing open
As another kyd starts to snore
Wham! In stomps a kyd holding a shoe
The soft gentle wisp of air
A sharp, harsh stinging sensation of
                                    a kyd being slapped
Scraping of the pencil sharpener
Another student tapping his pencil
Crack! Go stretching bones
The swishing of combs
All start to moan and groan to get ready
For another day awakens...passing time till we
                                         again go home.

[Age 12]

... *Personal Reflections*. . . . .

School

If you want to be a dude
   Have the right learning attitude!
You can have fun
   And still get your school work done.
Do you want to be a stud?
   Then don't think school is just a dud.
You have to be one with the crazy new fad...
   Don't think math is just something bad.
Are you one who wants to act hot & big;
   Then school has to be something you need to dig.
Stay in school and don't be dumb...
   Or someday you'll end up a homeless bum.
So as you can see...to be really "neat"
   Is to get in tune with the school beat!
Sometimes you'll drop
   And you'll want to give up and stop...
But find the strength to climb...until you rise...
   Soon you'll feel like you're one of the wise.
Be one of the "Really Cool,"
   Be smart..."Stay in School."

[Age 13]

... *Personal Reflections*. . . . .

What a Team!

As we dribble down the floor
We hear the fans screaming. . .
                        "Score - Score!"
We run and we run
Though we think the other team has won.

I was afraid I'd miss
Yet I flipped my wrist
Ten seconds left on the board
Until the opposing team wins the award.

The ball went in
So the game we did win.
Our faces still beam
Because we played as a team.

{Age 13]

. . . Personal Reflections. . . . .

Making a Difference

As he walked down the High School Hall
He saw the nasty words on the wall
Kids in chains
Students hanging around in gangs
Teachers afraid to go to class
Kids in the bathrooms smoking grass
It wasn't like twenty years ago
When days passed with an even flow
No writing on the walls
No gangs in the halls
No fighting
And no knifing
Just kids making phone calls
And studying in the halls
He changed the rules
And stopped the duels
He cleaned the walls
And cleared the halls
He chained the doors
And mopped the floors
He kicked the drugged kids out
And taught them what education was about
They soon all changed their way
And realized violence doesn't pay
Instead of fighting with each other
They learned to call each other "my brother"
Working together as a team
They learned what education, really does mean.

[Age 14]

. . . Personal Reflections. . . . .

["Seeing Eye to Eye" and "Heart and Soul" are dedicated to my brother with my love and admiration. You have been my leader, my protector & companion, my energy & strength, and my friend. I dedicate "The Pilot" and "Becoming One" to you and your fellow pilots. May you never lose sight of your dreams and always reach for the sky for it is that of a peaceful heart that makes those dreams come true.]

Seeing Eye to Eye

Though we don't always see eye to eye
We just can't deny...
That we are quite a pair
For all that we do and all that we share.

Even though we are always on the run
 Our hearts remain as one
You're my brother and inspiration to me
My friend for all eternity.

[Age 9]

. . . Personal Reflections. . . . .

Heart and Soul

A boy who was short and really quite small
Was considered a wimp by those so tall
No matter which way he'd walk
Nor which way he'd run
Classmates would talk and try to make fun.

But he didn't care
No matter how much they'd stare
Because though he didn't have the length
He made up for it with
His soul and inner strength.

This boy could listen
To what they would say
Day after day after day after day
Because whatever was said could not tear apart
My brother's gentle strength, his soul, and his heart.

[Age 12]

. . . Personal Reflections. . . . .

The Pilot

He can't wait to fly, up in the sky
For that is his lonely cry
He wants to fly for his great nation
So he's getting a good education.

He's going to be a Marine
To learn to be rough and lean
The Corps will teach him
Where fear leaves off, and strength begins.

I know the intention of my only brother
Is to save the lives of many others
By the sacrifice of his own
As his lonely flight embarks on the unknown.

[Age 15]

...Personal Reflections........

Becoming One

When a pilot steps into the cockpit
He becomes one with his plane
And as he quietly begins to sit
He suddenly feels no fear nor pain.

The plane slowly lifts off the ground
Soaring quickly into the sky
With earth's beauty falling all around
And hearing only...the eagle's cry.

He does not know what the future may hold
As he soars high above each new cloud
Yet even if the worst should begin to unfold
There is no complaint...for he is still proud.

The plane's wings sway like a mighty bird
As the pilot becomes one with his wings
No complaints are uttered...only silence is heard
For he knows the freedom his sacrifice brings.

[Age 13]

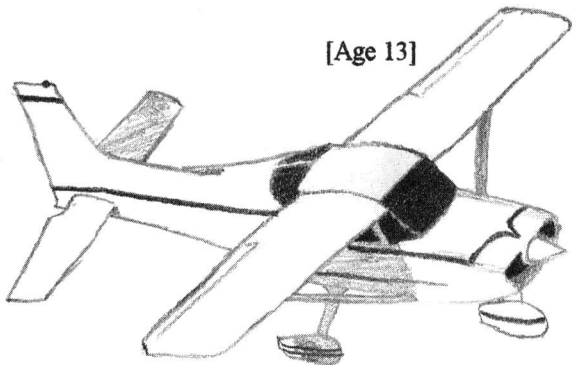

. . . Personal Reflections. . . . .

WHY?

I stand tall with pride.
They ask me; why?
When held high, I stand beside.
They ask me; why?

I hear its symbolic cry.
They ask me; why?
I know it's seen our soldiers die.
They ask me; why?

It represents the freedom we fight for.
They ask me; why?
Looking at America, it is the core.
They ask me; why?

It was made to be scared.
They ask me; why?
Now it's treated with hatred.
They ask me; why?

I place my hand over my heart.
They ask me; why?
When it's torn... I'm torn apart.
They ask me; why?

It's waving stripes gave us rights.
They ask me; why?
It's symbolic like the July 4th lights.
They ask me; why?

Freedom includes knowing to minimize speech.
They ask me; why?
Rights are earned, we much teach.
They ask me; why?

Will our country EVER learn?
They ask me; why?
A child sees it burn.
I ask them; WHY?

[Age 19]

. . . Personal Reflections. . . . .

Freedom

He walked by the water,
   Thinking of a dream.
A dream of many people...
   But what did it mean?

He ran through the forest,
   Looking for a dream.
A dream of many people...
   But what does it mean?

He sat alone on a stone,
   Thinking of a dream.
A dream called freedom...
   But what will it mean?

He stood before the people,
   Speaking of a dream.
He died for his freedom...
   And that is what it means!

[Age 15]

. . . Personal Reflections. . . . .

Peace

Exploding bombs and big invasions,
   many guns in a fight for glory.
So many have now lost their sons. . .
   yet another sad death story.

No more bombs and no more invasions;
   drop the guns and find real glory.
No more lost sons. . .
   and no more death stories.

Please save the world,
   is my lonely cry.
Try speaking instead of shooting. . .
   we can do it; if we try.

Join hands with nations around the world;
   drugs, terrorism, and war must cease.
Save the world is my crying plea. . .
   with just one word. . .and that is PEACE.

[Age 14]

. . . Personal Reflections. . . . .

Fight for Your Rights

There was a time among men
  When "free" was not a word
Rights were among the tyrants
  And voices were seldom heard.

We grew to learn of freedom
  In a land of opportunity
This land expanded rapidly
  With people from sea to sea.

We needed to name this glorious land
  That took Monarchy away
What better to call this place
  Than the good old U.S. A.

Yet times caused rebellion
  Against this loyal land
So in times of threat and war
  We must all take a stand.

In regard to our perpetual freedoms
  And rights of equality among men
We must be willing to defend them
  In any way we can.

We must uphold our freedoms
  No matter what the resulting cost
For a life without freedom
  Is an existence already lost.

[Age 15]

... *Personal Reflections*. . . . .

Keeping Score

I knew this man who went to war
To find the man who was keeping score
He went to tell him the war must cease
Because of course, he wanted peace.

The reason was a long time ago
He lost his dad in the big war show
He's still on his journey to find this man
Keeping score in green fatigues and his dark brown tan.

I hope he finds his man before another war
Or the man will be too busy keeping score
So let's hope he gets the score keeper to make peace
Then he'll make all of the other world wars cease.

[Age 10]

...Personal Reflections........

Thank You

As our men die left and right
They teach new kyds how to fight
Getting them ready to go to war
And telling them what's in store.

The kyds try to stand up tall
While they wan to hide from it all
As they get scared and want to cry
They watch their friends among them die.

They deserve way more than what they get
Fighting for men and kyds they have never met
For all they have done, they at least deserve two words
I just wish all the ones that are gone could have heard.

I'd just like to say *"Thank You!"*
It only makes my heart so very sad
That those who have died for our country
Couldn't hear those two words too.

[Age 11]

. . . Personal Reflections. . . . .

Celebrate Life

I walked past the cemetery the other day
It touched my heart in a special sort of way
I saw the tombs of the people who have died
I thought of those who have mourned and cried.

I guess we have got to be thankful and admit
If you really take time to think about it
Let's celebrate the time that we have got
It could be a little; or it could be a lot!

[Age 9]

The Gift

Since the very beginning of time,
God has made many gifts....
Some are big and some are small
Some are hidden and some stand tall
But there are two gifts that really stand out
With the miracle of peace and love
They are actually one and the same
One is a miracle, the other a name....
One gift comes from heaven above
The other comes from right here on earth
There was a Savior who gave Himself....
                                        for our strife
The other is our gift of life.

[Age 13]

...Personal Reflections........

Life's Shadow

Death is a shadow
That lingers behind our souls
Bringing dark thoughts to our minds...
Not knowing when it will be time to go

We spend our days with an eerie eye
Slowly watching every day...
Hoping we will be here for tomorrow
And missing the days gone by

So even as we think that death may be near
We are wasting our precious life away...
Not truly living our life
But dead... in a life of fear.

[Age 14]

Alone

Though I walk as one,
　I am not alone.
As water glistens
　from the rising sun;
I sit to enjoy life's beauty
　on a distant stone.

Sitting in silence on that stone,
　I look above
To say a quiet prayer...
　To my beloved Father
Looking down from heaven above.
　For He is always there
And I now know, I am never alone.

[Age 11]

. . . Personal Reflections. . . . .

God is There

As God's breath whispers across the land
Humans and nature join hand in hand...
And as God's tears fall to the ground
A magical rainbow is soon to be found.

Certainly God's smile brings about the light
As the sun peaks out, shining so bright...
But so does God's yell . . . move the sky
When his awesome lightening does fly.

Later God's night eye twinkles above
And you know he's still watching
                        . . . with lots of love
So when you go to bed tonight
Remember God is always there
                        . . .to hold you tight.

[Age 11]

. . . Personal Reflections. . . . .

One Day

The low mumble of a summer breeze
The ruffled crackling of swaying trees
Water moving at a roaming pace
I can't believe such a beautiful place.

The sun shining so bright above
A couple walks by...so much in love
Hand in hand along the shore
Falling in love...more and more.

As the sun slowly falls
With the night's gentle calls
Sunset appears...an awesome sight
The beautiful day turns into
                . . . a tranquil night.

[Age 15]

. . . Personal Reflections. . . . .

Be Not Afraid

Precious moments pass to eternity
So catch your dreams before they drift out to sea
But be not afraid
Just follow the path that God has made.

As your life changes and you go astray
Seemingly clear tat you've forgotten the way
Just be not afraid
And follow the path that God has made.

Don't linger on the troubled stones of your trail
For you must keep your soul warm,
                                      . . .not cold and frail
You cannot be afraid
To follow the path that God has made.

You must make a difference and take a stand
Leaving your footprints embedded in sand
You must not be afraid
As you follow the path that God has made.

So keep following His path, until its end
And as you turn back to recall all you've been
You need not be afraid
When you look back with pride...
                      on the life that you have made.

[Age 16]

. . . Personal Reflections. . . . .

A Child

A thunderous pounding fills my head
As the world turns dark around me
Lightening flashes startle me from behind
As the world turns dark around me.

A child screaming fills my ears
As the world turns dark around me
The river of pain fills my eyes with tears
As the world turns dark around me.

The child's pain-filled heart shows its wear
As the world turns dark around me
Will my world forever be sad and lonely
Will the world be forever dark around me?

Warmth touches my heart as a hand touches mine
A glimmer of light begins to calm me
A soft spoken word so gentle and kind
God's love turns the world bright around me.

[Age 12]

. . . Personal Reflections. . . . .

Closed Doors

As you walk through life's hallway
Getting scared more and more
Of what might come your way
As you close another door.

You can become a mourner
Of what you will see
Around the next corner
But remember what will be...will be.

For this world is made of much more
Than all the bad we've done
And remember after every closed door
God opens a new one.

[Age 10]

The Great Adventure
[Written for World Youth Day; Denver, Colorado, 1993]

Let's you and I take a ride
  With our hearts opened wide
To an experience we'll always share
  For together we can journey anywhere.

A journey of laughter, joy and smiles,
  With memories building over many miles
Meeting new people, faces and friends
  A book of memories that never ends.

Joining souls and faith with many nations
  Sharing our love of God's relations
This journey we take is a religious cure
  Known to us all, as *The Great Adventure!*

[Age 16]

... Personal Reflections........

Facts of Life

Death...
  It is so dark
Filled with sadness and pain
  So much hurt, yet no gain.

Then there's life...
  Which adds a spark
Filled with happiness and heart
  Like when you get a fresh new start.

Oh how I wish
  There was more Life than Death...
But I know it's not that way
  No matter what we do or say.

So let's be glad
  That we are alive...
Yet pray for those who are dying
  So they have a peaceful heart...I'm striving.

But most of all...
  Don't let the world get you down
And turn your frown around.

[Age 13]

. . . Personal Reflections. . . . .

The Mystery

I walk aimlessly in the night
Following the pale moonlight
Searching...
For a meaning of life's mystery.

Where did I get lost
Thinking of what wrong path I crossed
Wondering...
Of the meaning of life's mystery.

Still aimlessly walking alone
Waiting for me to be grown
Waiting...
For the meaning of life's mystery.

The sun rises to hear a bird sing
Suddenly as I walk along
Finding...
The beautiful meaning of life...
                no longer a mystery.

[Age 14]

... Personal Reflections........

That's What Life Is

The sun sets
Resting on the water
Ending the day peacefully

The sun rises above the trees
Showing a new beginning

The rain falling
Upon the animals that roam
It's dripping, dripping, upon the ground

Yet the snow
On the mountains
Is falling, falling all around

Then the morning dew
Makes the morning fresh
Not full of gloom and fog

Beauty is everywhere
East to west and from here to there
Because that's what life is!

[Age 12]

. . . Personal Reflections. . . . .

Nothing Less

Millions of people die each day
All in some different way
While we all sit and mope
We should learn to be positive and cope.

You'll never know until it happens to you
And there's nothing you, nor I, can do
Except fill your days with happiness
Nothing more...and nothing less.

[Age 14]

Life's Rollercoaster

It starts with beautiful pink and white lace
And a smile on everyone's precious face
Then there's the poverty, death and pain
That builds to a pulsating strain.

Then it slows down for a quick breath of air
And time for a little tender loving care
Or it could turn to an envious hate
As the heart starts to race at a raging rate.

Soon it calms down to a peaceful delight
With everything being so beautiful and bright
But then you slowly fade away
Until you wake to start another day.

[Age 15]

. . . Personal Reflections. . . . .

Daydreaming

[Dedicated to the little children who dream
of their own little perfect worlds. May
their hearts stay that way.]

I see a castle with elegant beauty and life
A unicorn dashes by with no sign of strife
As I look farther, I see the hills so big and green
A silver wolf sits on top of the hill, looking so keen.

Someone comes up and gives me a tap
Suddenly I wake up from my peaceful nap
My wonderful world comes to a quick end
There are no unicorns nor wolves around the bend.

But don't you wish our world were filled with beauty
Instead of war as everyone's duty
So daydreams could come true
For both me and you.

[Age 15]

... Personal Reflections........

Beauty

The mountains standing so tall and proud
As the sun's rays jump from cloud to cloud
Clouds crossing the bright blue skies
With the sound of people's laughs and cries.

The tap of the rain dancing on the ground
With the leaves ensemble sounding all around
The crisp, gentle flowing, clear air
A bird, with not a single care.

Though days have come and gone
The beauty of the world still lives on
Though changing in many ways
The beauty still forever stays.

[Age 15]

God's Rainbow

God made many beautiful people
That turned into selfish snobs
He made many things to do
Yet people still lose their jobs

God made every waterway
And now they are full of trash
He made the trees so they could sway
And we make them into ash

But there's one miracle that still gives us pleasure
With its beautiful color and glow
It's one important and permanent treasure
It is God's Rainbow

[Age 16]

. . . Personal Reflections. . . . .

Between the Raindrops

Between the raindrops are rays of sun
Leading to rainbows and summer days
Memories of things said and done
With paths leading to yesterdays.

Between the raindrops are times of bliss
Times remembered of tears that pour
And memories of storms that we don't miss
Yet those of bliss, we pray for more.

Between the raindrops, moments pass to memories
And agile days fade to tranquil nights
With a mist of history sending a chilling breeze
Of a time and life so fragile and slight.

Savor life, my friend, with all your heart
Though pain often lingers, don't give up and stop
Move on and remember, the pain too shall depart
And soon you will find rainbows...between the raindrops.

[Age 15]

... *Personal Reflections*. . . . .

Dreams

Keep your dreams close to your heart
And don't let people tear them apart
The ones that are new and some that are old
But mostly listen to your heart.....
                        where your dreams unfold.

Go for your goals, every day
No matter what people do, or say
Reach for your dreams. . .or at least try
But if you don't succeed . . . don't cry.

Just remember that you tried
And hold on to your self-pride
But don't forget that dreams do come true
And all they need is one thing. . . that is YOU!

[Age 14]

He'll Lift You Up

If you did something bad
And now you're really mad
Give it a rest
Just think...you tried your best
If everybody's mad at you
And there's nothing you can do
When you finally get ready to seek your doom
God lifts you up and heals your wound
He helps you through these long hard days
In so many different ways
Then you know you have an everlasting friend
Until the very, very end.

[Age 9]

...Personal Reflections........

The Honor of Dying

For years men have been dying
...for their country
...for their beliefs
...to be free.

A soldier dies for his country
...taking a lonely stand
...fear shown by his trembling hand
...sometimes on water, others on land.

A knight once fought for his palace
...with a sword, he rode across the land
...willing to die before dishonor
...in the palm of his enemies hand.

But one man died for His people
...without a shield, nor a sword
...He died with peace and tranquillity
...He is our Almighty Lord.

[Age 15]

. . . Personal Reflections. . . . .

Life

Her poignant face stared down at me
As tears filled her eyes
While she told me how life has to be
And her sadness turned to despise.

We talked about life from a distance
How it looks so beautiful and bright
And how that changes in an instance
To pain and scary fright.

She told me she wished life was always bright
And I told her we can change it easily
By first wanting to change the darkness to light
All we need is the strength between you and me.

[Age 15]

Memories

As you walk down that dirt road
You feel a shiver of the winter cold
You walk past the pond where minnows were sold
And the barn where stories were told.

Memories have come and gone...
                               at the end of that night
And a new day begins with the dawn
Days gone by are now stored neatly away
In a treasury of memories hidden out of sight.

[Age 13]

...Personal Reflections........

Dusting Off Dreams

Treasures of a childhood
Forsaken after time
Thoughts buried so deep
In a mind of endless rhyme.

A faithful youth's desire
For passions forgotten with age
Places and faces along life's journey
Fading into our history as just another page.

It's never too late
To see the light
Rekindle promises
Or to set things right.

Wake up my friend
And dust off those dreams
Cherish each precious moment
Knowing how much life means.

[Age 17]

. . . Personal Reflections. . . . .

I Think That I Shall Never See

...A guy who's perfect, just for me!
A man who is bright and doesn't bore me;
Who has the good taste to simply adore me.
...One who will make my insides tingle;
Who is (dare I hope) honest and single.
And who, if our lips should lock
...Can send my hormones into shock!
A man whose passion does not wane
When he finds out ...I have a brain.
...Yet one who will flatter, charm, and flirt
(A lot of money certainly couldn't hurt!)
So if you see my Mr. Right...
...Feel free to call me day or night.
And if Mr. Right doesn't come along
I'll maybe consider Mr. Wrong!

[Age 14]

. . . Personal Reflections. . . . .

Growing Up

For years my heart has been missin'
Something I've been searching for...
And now I realize I just had to listen.

Mom tried to tell me what was right
But I thought I knew it al...
Until it all hit me tonight.

She said an adult is more than independent
And adulthood doesn't guarantee strength...
Now I understand what she meant.

Growing up fast doesn't make a strong heart
Hurt any less than that of a child...
For that's when the real pain may start.

I now realize that not only has the past
Held me back from pursuing life...
But I have been wasting the present just as fast.

Growing up is not just getting old
But rather learning to stay young...
And enjoying life without being told.

[Age 18]

. . . Personal Reflections. . . . .

Miracles

Just when your world turns dim and gray
A beautiful rainbow rolls your way
And just as you feel your life on a fall
Something picks you up and stands you tall.

When you feel your future is certainly gone
A driving force pushes you to go on
And just as the pain seems there to stay
Something takes the pain away.

You come to what seems to be a dead end
But your problems are solved by the help of a friend
It doesn't matter who or how
Just that miracles are part of life. . . here and now.

[Age 14]

Strength

What *really* is strength?

Is it the length of distance we run...
Or could it be the amount of weight we can lift...
Perhaps it is the amount of heat from the sun...
Or the amount of drugs a lonely kyd sniffs?

Strength should not be measured in our height or weight...
Nor is it something visible by sight...
It doesn't even matter if we are six or sixty-eight...
Or if it is day nor night.

Strength comes from inside our heart...
Reaching out to others and lending a hand...
It helps us survive when we are near or far apart...
Being able to show we care...yet willing to take a stand.

[Age 10]

. . . Personal Reflections. . . . .

Feelings

Feelings are something we should not hide
You must not keep them deep down inside
A cub without its mother
Is a sadness like none other
But we must allow ourselves to feel the sorrow
Only feeling will allow healing tomorrow
Just as you must feel your happiness
Like a friend's smile or lover's caress
Just as a parent wipe's a falling tear
Allow your heart to cry out so others can hear.

[Age 10]

..... *just my thoughts*

Friends...

"Friends are people who care for and love you. Do you have a friend? They care and want to help you when you are feeling down. They sometimes want to cheer you up because they do not want to see you down and blue. So if your friends try to help you, put a little life in yourself and do not push your friends away."

Sharing...

"Sharing is something you can do with your family or friends. Sharing shows love. Friends are very special and they are very good at sharing cuz that's where friendship comes from is sharing. If we had no friends to share, what would we do? Would life be a bore or what? Life would be made of guns and fighting and no friendship at all."

[Age 7]

. . . Personal Reflections. . . . .

Heart of Gold

A bird falls down with a broken wing...
As a lover falls victim to a broken heart;
They both need someone with a "heart of gold"
Who will give them a gentle hand to hold.

The Heart of Gold helps pick up the pieces
With the lover...
As with the bird...
Without saying even a single word.

Soon the bird begins to fly...
As does the lover fall again in love.
With the help of someone with a heart of gold;
Patience and understanding, soon unfold.

There are no words to thank a Heart of Gold,
Nor even a way to repay it...
For all the hearts that it does mend,
We know of it only as ...a true "friend."

[Age 11]

... Personal Reflections........

The Peace-Keeper

We are all placed in a mold
That is stronger and much deeper
Than any conviction we hold...
I am the peace-keeper.

Everything has opposition
Because we all have our roles to play
We just never stop to listen...
To what everyone's role is today.

We do not get to choose our role
And it's yours 'till you meet your reaper
For it's our souls that he stole...
I am the peace-keeper.

I try my best to make amends
To the angered and the weeper
Hoping they see the message I send...
I am the peace-keeper.

The pain I live can never be seen
Because it must be held deeper
Than the pain I attempt to clean...
I am the peace-keeper.

We are all placed in a mold
That is stronger and much steeper
Than any conviction we hold...
And, I am the *peace-keeper!*

[Age 20]

. . . Personal Reflections. . . . .

I'll Be There

If the world crumbles at your feet
Or there's a load you cannot bare
Don't wait until you think you're beat
Tell me...I'll be there.

If there's something exciting and new
Or there's a secret you want to share
Don't wait until it bursts within you
Tell me...I'll be there.

If tears stream down and you're feeling weak
Or you just need someone to care
Don't wait until your life seems dark and bleak
Tell me...I'll be there.

If your inner soul wants to shine
Or you just want one to become a pair
A true friend has no time line
Tell me...I'll be there.

[Age 16]

My Friend

When you want to moan
And you feel like you're all alone
I'll be here....to wipe your tear
When you're no longer the class clown
And you're feeling down
I'll be there....because I care
When your tears fill up your cup
And you just want to give up
I'll stick by you....even while you are blue
We'll stick through thick and thin
For our battles we shall always win
I love you....and that is true
I'm going to be your friend until the very end!

[Age 12]

. . . Personal Reflections. . . . .

The Voice of Silence

Some say strength is shown through violence
But to many, violence is a choice
Not to show strength, but to break silence
Not to prove a point, but to have a voice.

Some say violence is a start
But destruction soon takes its toll
If the voice doesn't come from the heart
All communication loses its soul.

Still others say violence is a human fate
But death is not all fate is made of
For it is decided by the mistakes of hate
And determined by actions of love.

Until this message is heard
All hope is inevitably lost
Each of us must listen to the silent word
Or we all will suffer the fatal cost.

We must see that there is a choice
The way we express the thoughts we hold
Everyone has this silent voice
With each, their own story to be told.

We must learn and teach how to use this voice
Rather than using violence as a way out
This makes our actions our own choice
Leaving our mind free of all doubts.

Some say strength is shown through violence
But to many violence is still a choice
Not to show strength, but to break the silence
Not to prove a point, but to have a voice.

[Age 17]

...Personal Reflections.........

HOLLOW EYES

Outside you see
My sex, my age
You blame your actions
On my color, my wage. . .

You look down on me
As if you are wise
You stare at me
With your hollow eyes.

You hit me, beat me
And use your snapping words
You say **what** I am
Making me seen and not heard.

But I will not sit idol
And take your label
I have a voice
And I **am** able.

You should see
Hearts beat and tears fall
And fears and joys
Live in us all.

Stop looking at me
With your hollow eyes
And see the qualities
That give us ties.

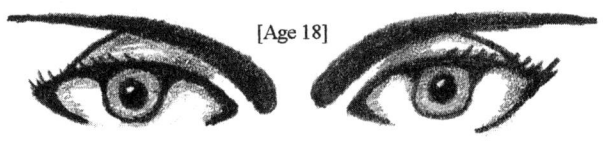

[Age 18]

. . . Personal Reflections. . . . .

A Silhouette

I saw a silhouette one night, as I lay fast asleep
The silhouette of a man I once knew; so many years ago.
Though I ran for his open arms; I could not reach...
For he was not for me to touch...
                      but rather a memory to keep.

This silhouette has an aura of days gone by;
A time with an equal bond that was so strong.
Now only our eyes are equal...
                      with the pain of stubborn pride,
As his silhouette fades and a tear falls from my eye.

Years later, I still dream of a man's silhouette;
The silhouette will sense the aura of days one by...
Helping to build our own strong bond...
Once again, I can smile and at least...
                      set my silhouette aside.

For though I may dream of this silhouette...
                      while fast asleep
The silhouette of a man I knew so many years ago...
No matter how hard I try, his arms I will never reach...
For he was not for me to touch,
                      but rather a memory to keep.

[Age 17]

. . . Personal Reflections. . . . .

Footprints On My Soul

It has been three years since you've died.
The pain still feels as though it was yesterday.

The pain feels like arthritis in my soul; yet hurts most when
spoken of or during special times of the year.

An open wound that tries to be healed, yet has no cure.

I wish I knew what was in your mind; while we stood in silence
with glares of hesitation.

So much should have, wanted, and needed to be said.
Yet nothing. . .the silence was deafening.

If only you could have helped me to understand.

We had so much in common, we even agreed on the denial of
our similarities.

I will never understand why you chose to leave. . .
*the questions have left **footprints on my soul**.*

I can only hope to move on and accept what I cannot change.

[Age 19]

. . . Personal Reflections. . . . .

Heavenly Friends

At the beginning, you were a stranger...
A man so big, with a face so full of life.
The one who protected me from all danger;
Watchful with eyes that frightened away my strife.

Then you were my Knight in shining armor...
A hero that could accomplish anything.
The one who taught me the words "madam" and "sir;"
Could run so fast as to soar on an eagle's wing.

But soon you became my worst enemy...
And childhood reality took a wrong turn.
Joy turned to sorrow when I saw you flee;
Teaching me one more thing...how to "crash and burn."

The call came in terror; and my heart just tore...
You have transformed from an enemy to a memory.
With tear-filled eyes, you knocked on heaven's door;
And once again reality has taken you away from me.

Yet as I speak to you now in silence...
I have learned we must forgive in order to mend.
So Dad, your message has finally been sent;
And someday...I hope that we're "heavenly friends."

[Age 17]

. . . Personal Reflections. . . . .

Silent Tears

With a smile she cries silent tears
With sparkles in her eyes, she hides her fears
Her big heart filled with pride
For her face has never been allowed to sigh
Full of darkness, yet showing a glimmer of light
During the day and throughout the night
Her face seems to glimmer. . .
                    like a radiant sunbeam
Yet deep inside, her tears realize it is. . .
                    only a dream.

[Age 17]

Star Wish

As I see a shimmering star
It looks so close, yet is so far away
A little ways away. . .I see the moon,
'Cause it will be getting dark soon.

I sat there for a little while
Feeling warm inside and starting to smile
As I think of our own human race
And all of the beauty we have in space.

Though I'm just a young teen
NOBODY understands what I've seen
'Cause I see things so differently. . .
The way things SHOULD be!

[Age 13]

. . . Personal Reflections. . . . .

Death's Shadow

Death is a shadow
That lingers behind our souls
Flashing deep thoughts on our minds
Not knowing when it will be time to go.

We spend our days with an eerie eye
Slowly watching. . . day by day
Hoping we'll be here for tomorrow
Yet missing the todays as they go drifting by.

So as we are thinking that death may be near
We are wasting our life away
Not truly living our life
But dead in a life of fear.

[Age 13]

. . . Personal Reflections. . . . .

My Heart Has No Ears

My eyes are colored mirrors
That lead deep into my soul. . .
They attempt to hide the fears. . .
As a thousand tears slowly roll.

        The mind says to move on
        But that never stops the tears. .
        A mind can scream from dusk till dawn. .
        My heart has no ears.

            Regrets begin to clutter the mind
            With images of past years. .
            I yell at what I see behind. .
            But my heart has no ears.

I've gained a lot of strength
From fighting off each tear. .
Though my mind has gone to great lengths. .
To make my heart hear.

        My mind is told to build a wall
        Preached to ignore emotion and fears. .
        To take the form of a plastic, smiling doll;
        Thank God, my heart has no ears.

            I can't hear the cry of hatred,
            Nor forget the pain of my years. .
            A pure soul, after all, is not wasted. .
            It's a blessing my heart has no ears.

[Age 19]

...Personal Reflections........

Hidden

In front of a mirror I stand
Analyzing the image I see
Just trying to understand
The reflection before me.

I ponder its significance
Over and over in my mind
Its pain I try to rinse
Attempting to leave the hurt behind.

The bottled emotion builds a shell
Imprisoning a little girl in chains
Forming a personal hell
Her tough pride taking the reigns.

With each passing year
Her tender heart is further hidden
I try to get her to shed a tear
Yet her shell makes it forbidden.

She comes across tough
But her heart is a rose
Afraid to be crushed if opened enough
So her shell forever grows.

[Age 19]

. . . Personal Reflections. . . . .

Destiny's Fool

An invisible fire burns
   around a heart with endless passion
Flaming a wall of inflammable tears
   inside a cluttered mind of fears.

As my mind takes lonesome walks
   to destinations only it does know
The fires solidify into rocks
   with time adding its own locks.

In order to find the keys
   one must believe in themselves
With emotions forgotten, I must use. . .
   I'm just wasting time, what could I lose?

I've lost so much with no choice
   while destiny played me for a fool
I must learn to trust in myself
   and put my fears upon the shelf.

[Age 16]

. . . Personal Reflections. . . . .

From a Distance

From a distance it's such a beautiful sight
Away from all the horror and fright
The softly flowing stream
As it slowly trickles with a gleam.

From a distance it's a precious smell
Away from all the trash, so it's easy to tell
The lovely smell of a fresh spring rose
How something can be so beautiful, only God knows.

[Age 15]

... *Personal Reflections*. . . . .

The Distant Dawn

My body is an earthquake
That shakes to my core
Causing my heart to ache
For what feels like ever more.

There are days of happiness
That give me some relief
But they're becoming less and less
Stolen by the sadness thief.

When the pain seems to have gone
An aftershock reappears
Making my mind distant of dawn
And closer to nighttime fears.

I must move on and enjoy my life
To avoid a natural disaster
Learning to control my own strife
Making me my own master.

[Age 18]

... *Personal Reflections*. . . . .

If Only

If Only I could see tomorrow...
Is it what I hope it to be?
If only I could prevent the sorrow...
Life has in-store for me.

If only I had a vision...
Where do I want to go?
If only I had a mission...
Of what I want to know.

If only I could find a destination...
Is this the road I should take?
If only I could find an explanation...
For all the questions I make.

If only I could be complete...
Is it a goal I can reach?
If only I could stop defeat...
Or learn what it has to teach.

If only I would stop crying...
Can I see if I am whole?
If only I would stop trying...
And see it is in my soul.

If only...

[Age 19]

. . . Personal Reflections. . . . .

BELIEVE
"words for thought..."

Belief is an abstract term that represents ones inner most hopes and convictions. Without it, life would be unbearable.

As children would believe in anything; every child hoped Santa Claus was real and believed sight unseen. Now as we grow older and our innocence fades, it becomes harder to believe. What use to be so simple has become very complex. Why is it easier to believe in Santa over ourselves? We need to look back at the innocence we once had, the hope we once saw, and the strength we once endured.

In order to succeed we must remember how to believe. Not in what is tangible or sure; but rather in the hopes and possible dreams in our souls. Learn not to believe in Santa Claus but in the hope and innocence he represents. Believe in yourself! Take your time; because, you are the greatest investment you will ever have. . .

If you ever feel alone and need a remainder of your strength and capabilities; know that I am right here beside you.....to support you and most of all....to believe in you.

[Age 20]

. . . Personal Reflections. . . . .

TRUE STRENGTH

WAR

    ENDURANCE

        AUDACITY

            KNOWLEDGE

NOBILITY

           EMPOWERS

      SUPPORT

   SOUNDNESS

With every great strength there is a weakness.
There is no greater sign of strength. . .
. . .than the courage to show weakness.

[Age 20]

... *Personal Reflections*. . . . .

My Life Sentence

How do I explain
What's weighing heavy on my soul
I have so much to gain
If my story is told.

I've been locked inside
For so many years
Trying to hide
My saddened tears.

Fear fills my mind
As hope fills my heart
I must stop walking blind
And begin a new start.

Can I escape from this hiding
With the pain you've helped me through
Why am I still deciding
If I should put my faith in you?

Could I justly be sentenced
To a life of suspicion
Of any kind person
My heart tries to listen?

[Age 18]

. . . Personal Reflections. . . . .

My Mission

I cannot change the world,
But I can change how I live in it.
I cannot see tomorrow,
But I can accomplish any vision today.

I won't always be first,
And no one is ever perfect.
I can't change my mistakes;
But I can grow and learn from each one.

I can't change tomorrow
But I can make today go right.
I can't avoid trouble in my way;
But I can stand and give it a fight.

[Age 19]

. . . Personal Reflections. . . . .

My Personal Mission Statement

Faith

Honesty

Pride

Honor

LOVE

Patience

Respect

Trust

Soul

Mind

Possibilities

... all in me !

[Age 20]

. . . Personal Reflections. . . . .

One

There is only one person
that can make me cry...
wipe that same tear,
and make me try.

There is only one person
that can make me mad...
calm those fears,
and make me glad.

There is only one person
that can make me fall...
give me the vision,
to proudly stand tall.

There is only one person
that is my guide...
and I've made the decision
to look inside.

There is only one person
that can make me be
who I am
and that *one* is me!

[Age 19]

. . . Personal Reflections. . . . .

Is A Valentine...

...A fresh rose, grown in the wild
With the smell of the morning dew?
Is it the birth of a newborn child;
Or is it just saying: "I Love You?"

Can it be the sight of the clear blue sky,
As the sun makes the earth glow?
Could it be the twinkle in someone's eye;
Or does only God really know?

It could be the feeling of someone's touch;
Whether it be that of a hand or a heart...
All of these can mean so very much,
If only they could be shared from the start

...Yet even when clouds form in our sky above,
And the sunshine fades away...
The linger of that touch of love
Will be there always to stay !!!

A Valentine is .... Heart - to - Heart !

[Age 16]

. . . Personal Reflections. . . . .

Love

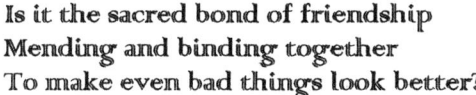

What is love?

Is it the sacred bond of friendship
Mending and binding together
To make even bad things look better?

Is it never having to say you're sorry
To a friend or a loved one
No matter what you've done?

Is it sharing all your emotions
All the fears
And the many tears?

Or is love just a word
We just use day to day
That we can take, or give away?

Well actually, love is all of these
Because you see
Love is whatever you make it be!

[Age 14]

. . . Personal Reflections. . . . .

I Love You

[Dedicated to Tanner]

I never knew how much I could love,
    Until I met you.
I never gazed with wonder at the stars above
    Until I met you.

I never believed in following dreams
    Until I met you.
I never knew my heart could silence its scream
    Until I met you.

I never knew someone so gentle and kind
    Until I met you.
I never met a guy who totally blows my mind
    Until I met you.

I never felt I could conquer all strife
    Until I met you.
You gave me the gift of a bright new life
    And for that "I love you."

[Age 20]

...Personal Reflections........

A Small Price to Pay
[Written for my first true love - TJF]

Money doesn't matter
  When beauty has begun...
And the rays begin to scatter
  Into a setting sun.

Imagine if what I love so much,
  Was sold in every store.
I couldn't even afford to touch
  These beauties anymore.

The sparkle in your eyes,
  Would cost quite a few...
With the colors of the skies
  And purity so true.

The fortune in your smiles,
  Would buy any nation;
Stretching across the miles...
  Like a heavenly creation.

There are so many pieces
  In you, to love and desire.
Just think of all the leases,
  I'd have to acquire.

It's a glorious blessing to me,
  Not to have to pay...
For all the pleasures I see
  In this beautiful world today.

Because to me, your touch is gold,
  And I'd gladly go in debt...
To be the one you hold
  At every sunset.

[Age 20]

. . . Personal Reflections. . . . .

Grace

I wish grace was everywhere
I hope the sun forever shines on our glorious land
Someday I hope another's grace will shine down onto me.

I love it when someone else lets their grace shine through
For everyone needs to open their heart and enjoy life.

Grace is what your heart releases
When you ride the rollercoaster of life
But if you listen to your heart,
                your grace will guide you through.

[Age 8]

I Am

I am a life lover
I wonder what tomorrow will bring
I hear the tranquil trees a swaying
I see the ocean flowing
I am a life lover.

I pretend that I can change the world
I feel a crisp but gentle breeze
I touch the silk-like-flowers
I worry about poverty and death
I cry about all the terror and pain
I am a life lover.

I understand no one person can change the world
I say all we can do is to try to keep smilin'
I dream of peace across the great oceans and lands
I try to do my share
I hope I can do enough
I am a life lover.

[Age 13]

... *Personal Reflections*........

One More Day

Today the world is viewed in black and white
  With not a rainbow color in sight
The snow is all melted, making room for rain
  Decorating my car with an earthy stain.

The smell is fresh and new
  With a light wind, where the birds once flew
A calm silence hovers over the land
  Giving thoughts of relief, summer and sand.

Spring is truly on its way
  We know now, from this dreary day
A few more steps in the shimmering snow
  And these winter times will surely go.

[Age 17]

Fall

Fall is when the leaves come falling down
  Colors, sizes, and shapes so rare
Coming down with colors yellow, orange, and brown
  Until all the trees are so bare.

It is fun to jump into piles of leaves
  Laughing and playing with your friends
Finally pulling the leaves off your sleeves
  But wishing the fun would never end.

[Age 8]

. . . Personal Reflections. . . . .

Winter

The sky darkens...
As the land begins to freeze
Into hibernation...
With a gentle, flowing breeze.

Little white parachutes
Falling slowly to the ground
With shimmering white snowflakes
Dancing all around.

Now a white blanket
Lays peacefully on the ground
Resting in hibernation
Without a single sound.

Children get bundled
To play in the snow
Playing 'till they feel frozen
Why.......we don't know.

Then the sun awakes
To make the new day bright
Shining on the snow
It is such a beautiful sight.

The sun keeps glowing
Melting the snow away
Now there's just water
And no snow for us to play.

Soon it will be time for T-shirts
And playing on the lawn
Days are getting longer
For winter has come and gone.

[Age 8]

. . . Personal Reflections. . . . .

Trees

Trees are the greatest things I know
They do no harm, they just grow and grow
They make shade for the sleepy cows
And are a shelter for our little bird house.

Some trees give us fruit to eat
Their wood we burn to give us heat
The wood we make our houses of
Is from the trees on we once did love.

In 1865 a great man did say
It is time we have an Arbor Day
Everyone can plant a tree
Everybody....including me.

Children all over our great land
Can join together, hand in hand
To learn the beauty and learn to see
Just how important a tree can be.

So let's remember this Arbor Day
In a very special way
By planting a tree and helping it grow
Because trees are the best things I know.

[Age 12]

. . . Personal Reflections. . . . .

A Winter's Frost

Fall is finally done
With the last drop of golden sun
Days and nights turning cold
As we find someone warm to hold.

Leaves are off all the trees
As the land begins to freeze
In the woods is a mother doe
Trying to let her baby go.

The sudden shot of a gun
Sends the deer out to run
The baby still was very small
It didn't have a chance at all.

The ending of her life will bring
New days turned into spring
But saddened of the doe that is lost
A cold, hard memory of the winter's frost.

[Age 9]

. . . Personal Reflections. . . . .

Serenity

Precious purple sky
  Blend into disarray
    Orange clouds
      That move like busy bees

      Flowing waves brush
        Quietly onto the shore
          With the silent song
            Of a bird flying by

            An orange and white
              Fireball rest on the red
                Horizon like flames
                  With its colorful glow.

    All ends with
      Serenity and tranquil
        Beauty of our wonderful
          And extraordinary world.

[Age 12]

. . . Personal Reflections. . . . .

Upon a Star

I once wished upon a star
For something just as bright...
Filling me with just as much
Joy as this star each night.

This wish was not a miracle
Or a hardworking task...
Just a favor put toward the sky
Not too big for one to ask.

I just wish for love
Even if it is from a falling star...
Something pure and true as the stars
Right now seeming just as far.

Someday, I pray a star will fall
Only this time into my arms...
For me to cherish and to love
With all his faults and charms.

Just the thought of someone to love;
To share the star that shines so bright...
Sharing our life both good and bad
With the rush of day and peace of night.

Is that wish too much to ask?
To be happy and not alone...
To have love and joy...
Is this wish so unknown?

Yes, I once wished upon a star
For something just as bright...
Filling me with just as much joy
As this beautiful star each night.

[Age 19]

. . . Personal Reflections. . . . .

Never Say Good-bye

As our eyes fill with tears
You quietly begin to cry
Our minds think of the last few years
And I wipe the tear from your eye.

You say you wish we didn't have to go our own ways
Soon we both begin to cry
We promise to write and share our days
But never, ever say good-bye.

We pledge our friendship forever
Whether together or far apart
Our bond no one will dare sever
For it is buried deep within our hearts.

[Age 13

...Personal Reflections........

Moving On . . .

How can one say good-bye
To those they love so much. . .
But to hold their head up high
With a smile, trying not to cry.

Our lives are filled with paths to take
With no certainty of their length. . .
So we look ahead with joy and faith
For it's a journey we all must make.

A path of wonder and sights to see
To which we know not the end. . .
Our spirits high and full of dreams
Only God holds the future to be.

So though my time has come to depart
And I'll miss you all immensely. . .
I will take this road paved just for me;
Your memories and love in my heart.

[Age 17]

... *Personal Reflections*. . . . .

Don't Let it Go Unsaid...

At the age of 20, Amy Rose decided that not another day would go by without telling the special people in her life how they had touched her heart. As a matter of healing for all of the loses she had endured, she wrote letters telling the people in her life what they meant to her. Those of you; whether family, friends, or passing acquaintances, whom Amy's life has touched, know who you are and it is her love and admiration for all of you that has inspired this book. *You* know who you are.

... Exerpts from the writings of Amy Rose...

...... *"It's not what one does for or gives someone that means the world or develops the memory. It is the time and emotions presented that creates that memory.*

...... *I have lived a life that I wish upon no one; but I also can say that I have lived a life that I would trade with no one. I have suffered; but I have also survived. I have lost many; but also have loved many. I have forgotten so much; but remember even more. I may not be able to say I was the most popular or prettiest or talented; but I can honestly say that I was loved and enjoyed life to the utmost.*

...... *I feel that the trauma and hardship I have been through has made me a stronger person. The struggles in my life have made me want to fight harder to achieve my dreams and goals. I believe God gave me these obstacles for a reason and I will not allow these struggles to have a negative effect on my life. I see now that joy can only come from us seeing through the pain in life. Without it, happiness would have no meaning.*

. . . Exerpts Continued. . .

. . . . . . So many things have happened to me in my life that I can't change or forget, but with those memories come knowledge and strength. I could sit here and say I wish that none of them ever happened but that would just deny who I am today. Every struggle that I confronted was just another that I overcame. With each obstacle overcome, insight and strength was won. The best I can do is take these "battles won" and learn from them."

Don't let your feelings go "unsaid." Tell the special people in your life how you feel about them, how they have inspired your life, or how they have touched your heart. We know not what tomorrow will bring, so be thankful for the gift of each precious new day and share the love in your heart with those you love.